W9-BIX-012

J PAR STORYTIME KIT REP 2

Reptiles: snap, slither & slime [storytime kit]
Total - 12 pieces
31112018411179

Gila Monsters/
Monstruos de Gila

By JoAnn Early Macken

Reading Consultant: Jeanne Clidas, Ph.D.
Director, Roberts Wesleyan College Literacy Clinic

WEEKLY READER®
PUBLISHING

Please visit our web site at **www.garethstevens.com**.
For a free catalog describing our list of high-quality books,
call 1-877-542-2595 (USA) or 1-800-387-3178 (Canada).
Our fax: 1-877-542-2596

Library of Congress Cataloging-in-Publication Data

Macken, JoAnn Early, 1953–
    [Gila monsters. Spanish & English]
    Gila monsters = Monstruos de gila / by JoAnn Early Macken; reading consultant, Jeanne Clidas.
       p. cm. — (Animals that live in the desert = Animales del desierto)
    Includes bibliographical references and index.
    English and Spanish; translated from the English.
    ISBN-10: 1-4339-2062-X   ISBN-13: 978-1-4339-2062-2 (lib. bdg.)
    ISBN-10: 1-4339-2457-9   ISBN-13: 978-1-4339-2457-6 (soft cover)
    1. Gila monster—Juvenile literature. 2. Lizards—-Juvenile literature. I. Title. II. Title: Monstruos de gila.
  QL666.L247M33318   2010
  597.95'952–dc22
                                        2009009780

This edition first published in 2010 by
Weekly Reader® Books
An Imprint of Gareth Stevens Publishing
1 Reader's Digest Road
Pleasantville, NY 10570-7000 USA

Copyright © 2010 by Gareth Stevens, Inc.

Executive Managing Editor: Lisa M. Herrington
Senior Editor: Barbara Bakowski
Cover Designers: Jennifer Ryder-Talbot and Studio Montage
Production: Studio Montage
Translators: Tatiana Acosta and Guillermo Gutiérrez
Library Consultant: Carl Harvey, Library Media Specialist, Noblesville, Indiana

Photo credits: Cover, p. 17 Shutterstock; pp. 1, 13 © Lynn M. Stone; pp. 5, 9, 21 © John Cancalosi/
naturepl.com; p. 7 © Jeff Foott/naturepl.com; p. 11 © Joe McDonald/Visuals Unlimited;
pp. 15, 19 © Jim Merli/Visuals Unlimited

Printed in the United States of America

1 2 3 4 5 6 7 8 9 14 13 12 11 10 09

Table of Contents

- - - - - - - - - - - - - -

Contenido

Boldface words appear in the glossary./
Las palabras en **negrita** aparecen en el glosario.

Giant Lizard

The Gila (HEEL-ah) monster is a lizard. It is the largest lizard that lives in the United States. Its bite has poison called **venom**.

- - - - - - - - - - - - - -

Un lagarto gigantesco

El monstruo de Gila es un lagarto. Es el lagarto más grande de Estados Unidos. Su mordedura es **venenosa**.

5

Lizards are **reptiles**. They move into the sun to warm up. They hide in the shade to stay cool.

- - - - - - - - - - - - - -

Los lagartos son **reptiles**. Se ponen al sol para calentarse. Se esconden en la sombra para refrescarse.

7

Gila monsters live in the **desert**. They hide most of the time. In the summer, they rest under the ground. In the winter, they **hibernate**, or sleep.

- - - - - - - - - - - - - -

Los monstruos de Gila viven en el **desierto**. La mayor parte del tiempo están escondidos. En el verano, descansan bajo tierra. En el invierno **hibernan**, es decir, duermen.

9

The Gila monster is covered with **scales**. The scales look like beads. Some scales are black. Some are pink or orange.

- - - - - - - - - - - - - -

El monstruo de Gila está cubierto de **escamas**. Las escamas parecen bolitas. Algunas son negras. Otras son rosadas o anaranjadas.

scales/
escamas

The Gila monster has strong claws. Its tongue is purple. The tip is forked, or split into two points.

- - - - - - - - - - - - - - -

El monstruo de Gila tiene fuertes garras. Su lengua es de color morado. La punta de la lengua es bífida, es decir, está dividida en dos.

claws/
garras

tongue/
lengua

13

Meals for a Monster

Gila monsters have sharp teeth. They eat eggs from birds, snakes, and turtles. They also eat small animals.

- - - - - - - - - - - - - - -

Comidas de monstruo

Los monstruos de Gila tienen dientes afilados. Se comen los huevos de pájaros, serpientes y tortugas. También comen animales pequeños.

A Gila monster can eat a huge meal. It may not eat again for a long time. It stores fat in its tail. Later, it lives on the fat.

- - - - - - - - - - - - - - -

Un monstruo de Gila puede comer mucho de una vez. Después es capaz de no volver a comer en largo tiempo. Almacena la grasa en su cola. Luego, vive de esa grasa.

tail/
cola

Strong From the Start

Female Gila monsters lay eggs in the sand. The eggs stay warm in the sun. Babies hatch from the eggs. The babies have teeth and venom.

- - - - - - - - - - - - - - -

Fuertes desde el principio

Las hembras ponen sus huevos en la arena. Los huevos se calientan con el sol. Las crías salen de los huevos. Las crías tienen dientes y veneno.

babies/
crías

eggs/
huevos

19

If a Gila monster is scared, it tries to back away. It may even open its mouth and hiss. If it cannot escape, it may bite!

- - - - - - - - - - - - - -

Cuando se asusta, un monstruo de Gila trata de huir. Es posible que abra la boca y emita un sonido sibilante. Si no consigue escapar, ¡puede morder!

Fast Facts/Datos básicos

Length/ Longitud	about 2 feet (61 centimeters) nose to tail/ unos 2 pies (61 centímetros) de nariz a cola
Weight/ Peso	about 4 pounds (2 kilograms)/ unas 4 libras (2 kilogramos)
Diet/ Dieta	small animals, frogs, birds, and eggs/animales pequeños, ranas, pájaros y huevos
Average life span/ Promedio de vida	up to 30 years/ hasta 30 años

Glossary/Glosario

desert: a dry area with little rainfall

hibernate: to go into a deep sleep for a long time

reptiles: animals that breathe air, have a backbone, and usually have scales or bony plates on their bodies

scales: thin, flat plates that cover the bodies of snakes, fish, and other animals

venom: poison

- -

desierto: zona seca donde cae poca lluvia

escamas: placas delgadas y planas que cubren el cuerpo de las serpientes, los peces y otros animales

hibernar: permanecer en un sueño profundo durante mucho tiempo

reptiles: animales que respiran aire, tienen columna vertebral y suelen tener el cuerpo cubierto de escamas o placas óseas

venenoso: que contiene veneno

For More Information/Más información

Books/Libros

Gila Monsters. Early Bird Nature Books (series). Conrad J. Storad (Lerner, 2007)

What Desert Animals Eat/¿Qué comen los animales del desierto? Nature's Food Chains (series). Joanne Mattern (Gareth Stevens, 2006)

Web Sites/Páginas web

Gila Monster/Monstruo de Gila

animals.nationalgeographic.com/animals/reptiles/ gila-monster.html
Watch a short video about a Gila monster./Vean un video corto de un monstruo de Gila.

Gila Monster/Monstruo de Gila

www.whozoo.org/anlife2000/jamiebritt/gilaindexrev.html
Read all about the Gila monster. See cool photos, too./ Conozcan todos los detalles sobre el monstruo de Gila y vean fotografías asombrosas.

Publisher's note to educators and parents: Our editors have carefully reviewed these web sites to ensure that they are suitable for children. Many web sites change frequently, however, and we cannot guarantee that a site's future contents will continue to meet our high standards of quality and educational value. Be advised that children should be closely supervised whenever they access the Internet.

Nota de la editorial a los padres y educadores: Nuestros editores han revisado con cuidado las páginas web para asegurarse de que son apropiadas para niños. Sin embargo, muchas páginas web cambian con frecuencia, y no podemos garantizar que sus contenidos futuros sigan conservando nuestros elevados estándares de calidad y de interés educativo. Tengan en cuenta que los niños deben ser supervisados atentamente siempre que accedan a Internet.

Index/Índice

About the Author

JoAnn Early Macken is the author of two rhyming picture books, *Sing-Along Song* and *Cats on Judy*, and more than 80 nonfiction books for children. Her poems have appeared in several children's magazines. She lives in Wisconsin with her husband and their two sons.

- - - - - - - - - - - - - -

Información sobre la autora

JoAnn Early Macken ha escrito dos libros de rimas con ilustraciones, *Sing-Along Song* y *Cats on Judy*, y más de ochenta libros de no ficción para niños. Sus poemas han sido publicados en varias revistas infantiles. Vive en Wisconsin con su esposo y sus dos hijos.